# THE
# BITTERSWEET OZARKS
# AT A GLANCE

# THE BITTERSWEET OZARKS AT A GLANCE

by

Ellen Gray Massey

Photography by the staff of *Bittersweet, the Ozark Quarterly*

Publisher:      Skyward Publishing, Inc
                Dallas, Texas
                Marketing:  813 Michael Street
                Kennett, MO  63857
                Phone (573) 717-1040
                Fax:  413-702-5141
                E-Mail:  skyward@semo.com
                Website:  www.skywardpublishing.com


Printed in China


Photo credit: page. 2—Mike Doolin and Stephen Ludwig on the Osage Fork River. Photo by Daniel Hough.

**Library of Congress Cataloging-in-Publication Data**

The Bittersweet Ozarks at a glance / [compiled] by Ellen Gray Massey ;
photography by the staff of Bittersweet, the Ozark quarterly.
    p. cm.
  ISBN 1-881554-23-6
  1.  Ozark Mountains Region—Social life and customs. 2.  Ozark Mountains Region—Description
and travel. 3.  Ozark Mountains Region—Pictorial works.  I. Massey, Ellen Gray. II. Bittersweet.
    F417.O9 B59 2003
    976.7'1—dc21

                                              2003004827

To the one hundred and six students whose enthusiasm,
curiosity, talents, and dedicated work created
*Bittersweet, the Ozark Quarterly* for all to
understand and appreciate their American heritage.

# ACKNOWLEDGMENTS

Thanks to the many men and women who let us into their homes and their lives to share with us their heritage.

Special thanks to Central Bank of Lebanon, Missouri, for continual support over the years and financial assistance in publishing this book; to the Mapplethorpe Foundation of New York also for help in publishing; and the Lebanon Publishing Company of Lebanon, Missouri, for support from our beginning in 1973.

# CONTENTS

Photo 2
"Those were days that you kids will never know." Clarice Splan

# FOREWORD

It is not often that high school students can do anything to preserve their heritage. The followers of fashion and current trends, they have traditionally been labeled as disinterested in the past and as rebels against family and school authorities attempting to continue the status quo. This is especially true in rural areas or small towns such as Lebanon, Missouri, population less than 10,000, where the young people often leave the area as soon as they graduate.

As a teacher in several small schools in south central Missouri, I recognized these trends which were even more pronounced in the Ozarks because of many years of media stereotyping of its people. Taught by comic books and other media coverage that the region is backward, lazy, half-clothed, and ignorant, young people often became ashamed of their background.

But they also knew the picture was unfair. Everywhere they looked they saw hard-working men and women. They came from church-going families with strict moral standards. They knew how intelligent the people were, how witty, and friendly.

But when they traveled or came into contact with other people, sometimes including their teachers from outside the area, their speech was ridiculed, their family customs belittled. Since most youth want to emulate their national peer group, they tried to conform. Though inwardly proud of their beautiful, hilly countryside, their running streams, and other natural wonders, they would not let on where they were from. Once away from the area, most tried to eliminate any trace of their background.

This behavior is what I observed up into the 1970s when I initiated a course in Ozark studies. Students' self worth increased as they studied the unique geological formations of their land, as they understood the history of the early settlers in the area, and learned the true character of the Ozarks—how their forebearers, right down to their own parents, worked to create a living and a society based on individual initiative coupled with neighborly help and support.

From this class developed a language arts course, the students named Bittersweet. Its purpose was two-fold: (1) The students learned by publishing and promoting a magazine about the Ozarks. By doing so they experienced many facets of communication—oral history and library researching, writing, revising, photography and other illustrations, layout, promotion, speaking, as well as interactions with their peers, the men and women whom they interviewed, and their reading public. As the students were learning these and other business and leadership skills, they were performing a needed service. (2) The young people were preserving the knowledge and lore—the way of life in the Ozarks.

It is now almost thirty years since the first students began their work. Had they not researched and recorded, the information from the 494 men and women they captured in words and pictures would be lost forever, for most of them have died. From 1973 until 1983 the young people published 482 articles and features in 40 issues of *Bittersweet, the Ozark Quarterly*. Though now the magazine is available to the public only in libraries (also on-line at the Springfield-Greene Country Library in Springfield, Missouri— orion.org), some of these stories have been included in two anthologies, *Bittersweet Country* and *Bittersweet Earth*, University of Oklahoma Press.

The students' objective to preserve their culture continues with the publication of this book of photographs. Designed to give newcomers to the Ozarks a glance at the true character of the Ozark Plateau and its people, it is also a book for Ozark natives to reminisce proudly as they tie together the many facets of their background.

No, it is not often that high school students can do anything to preserve their heritage. Seldom do they team up with their families and teachers to understand the existing society. But that is exactly what the Bittersweet students did with their research and writings and with the 49,265 photographs they shot and filed. Following are some sample pictures that I have selected to illustrate *The Bittersweet Ozarks at a Glance*.

Ellen Gray Massey

Photo 3
The bittersweet vine, a symbol of the color and endurance of the Ozarks and its people. Coming into its beauty after all other fall color is gone, if kept in a dry place, it will keep for years.

# PROLOGUE

Persistence and change. Opposites describe the Ozarks and its people. Wild and cultivated. Isolated and in the news. Or perhaps maligned yet much sought after. There is a homogeneity that disguises its variety and complexity.

The dichotomy of the Ozarks is evident throughout its history and everywhere you look today. Poor ridges and rich stream valleys. Lush woods and arid rocky glades. Steep hills and flat prairies. A living that is bitter and sweet. Traditionally independent, self-sufficient, and clannish, its people have resisted change, yet the area is one of the fastest growing and most visited in the United States. Though ignored and ridiculed for years because of its rough, inaccessible terrain, and the post-frontier living style of its people, it is now, because of these very features, a haven for retirees and young couples seeking a better place to raise their families.

The land and its people persist. In spite of the changes, you can still catch a glimpse of the past. In the present you can understand how that past may influence the future.

*The Bittersweet Ozarks at a Glance* is about the land, how the people who settled here used the land, and the life style they created on the Ozark Plateau.

Photo 4
A high bluff of the Niangua River above Bennett Spring overlooks a quiet eddy and acres of oaks, maples, and other deciduous trees crowding the river banks and covering the hills. A scene similar to this can be seen on almost any of the many streams in the Ozarks of southern Missouri and northern Arkansas.

# ONE

# THE LAND

Photo 5
A herd of pink Elephant Rocks seems to march over the crest of this mountain near Graniteville in Iron County. Dumbo, the largest, weighs about 680 tons. It has taken one and a half billion years of first uplifts and then erosion to mold these giants.

# THE LAND

The oldest geological formation of any size in the United States, the Ozark Plateau is characterized by rocks, water, and trees. The underlying igneous rocks (granite) are covered by sedimentary limestone from animal shells and calcium deposited from the seas that periodically covered the area. For over 300 million years, there have been uplifts and erosion. The latest uplift fifty million years ago raised the 60,000 square mile plateau above the surrounding lands. Wind and water then carved out the valleys and rounded off the tops of the more resistant hills which were the floor of the original plateau. Trees and other vegetation covered the land. As water continues to seep through the ground, it becomes slightly acidic and eats passageways through the limestone, forming a honeycomb of underground caves and waterways. Some of these channels emerge as springs to feed the many surface rivers and creeks.

Like grassy fingers thrust into the dissected forested hills, some large areas that have resisted erosion developed into savannahs and prairie tracts.

The human settlers found a rocky, well-watered land, lush with vegetation and populated with many wild animals.

Photo 6
What water has accomplished is easier to see in this photograph where the Black River has carved its way through the granite to form Johnson's Shut-Ins.

# ROCKS AND WATER

Rocks and water. Two opposites that give form and life to the Ozarks. Sterile and unyielding, extending to the center of the earth, rocks are solid, hard, and inert. Rocks impede growth and inhibit movement. Can anything be more powerful than rocks? Life-giving, free-flowing, freezing and thawing, drop by drop, water attacks rocks, wearing them down, dissolving its way into their core and carving passages through them. Over eons water grinds mammoth formations into fine sand which it deposits in low places to develop soil. Surely nothing is more powerful than water.

Photo 7

⇐ Can you imagine eons ago the Niangua River as a young rivulet on the top of this bluff? That's where this tranquil-looking stream began its unending labor to dissect the area into hills and valleys.

Photo 8

⇑ Natural bridges are common along the waterways. The more resistant arch remains while its underpinnings have been eaten away.

Photo 9

⇑ Water gives and takes. This sycamore is dependent for sustenance and anchorage from the soil deposited in the rich bottom land of the Osage Fork of the Gasconade River. A few more seasons will see the river take away those life supports.

Photo 10

⇒ Some springs in the Ozarks are among the largest in the world. No one knows for sure how many there are. Over 1,100 have been recorded in Missouri alone. In some springs the underground water comes to the surface bubbly and effervescent.

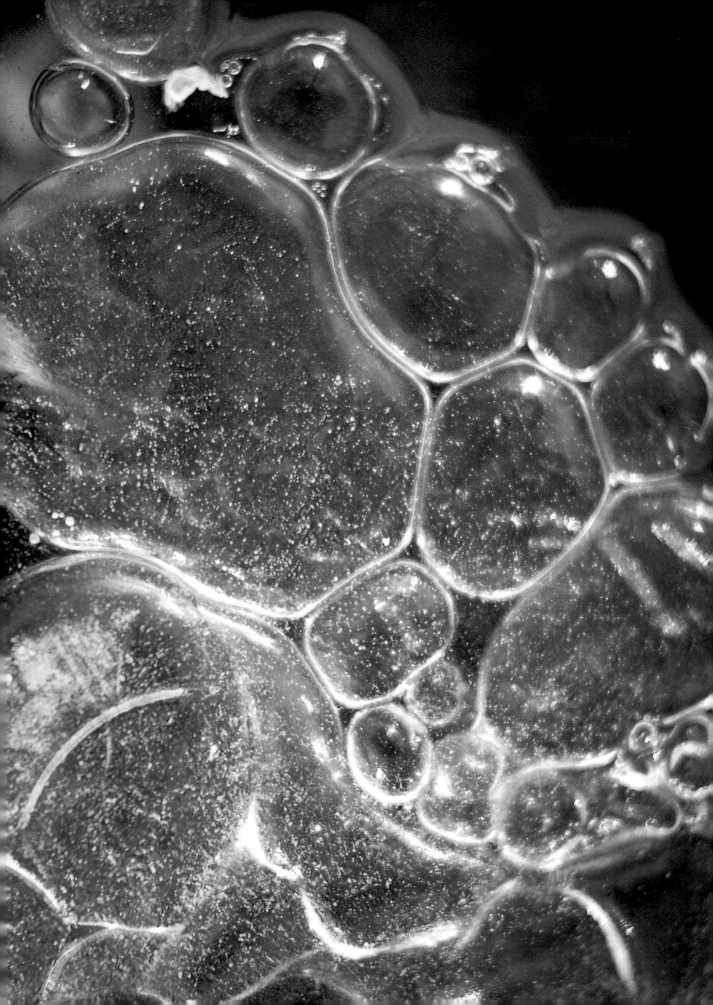

Photo 11
⇐ Other springs gush out, cascading over the rocks, cooling (or warming) the surrounding air with its constant temperature of about 58 degrees.

Photo 12
⇑ Much of water's work is hidden below the surface. Seepage from above and underground currents carve out rooms, sculpting beautiful and varied formations.

Photo 13
⇑ Frequently the dissolving force of the water on the rocks is so great that the roof of the cavity falls in, creating dangerous sinkholes.

Photo 14
⇒ At Grand Gulf in Oregon County the roof of a long passage fell in forming a mini-canyon that sometimes holds water.

Photo 15

⇐ But in another place and time the water's constant movement on rocks can be purely aesthetic when it is frozen to a temporary stop.

Photo 16

⇑ Even in frigid winter when all moisture is frozen, warm spring waters trickle among the rocks down through the woods . . .

Photo 17A
⇑ . . . to make a brief temperature change in the ice-coated river.

Photo 17B
⇒ A few weeks will change the river scene. Flowering dogwood edges the river with a different kind of white.

Photo 18

APRIL'S SEDUCTION

Bright April's sensuality
                seduces me.
              The scented breeze
              and sun's warmth seize,
enfold, caress me. I succumb.
              And I become
              the melodies
              of birds and bees,
the redbud, mosses, daffodil,
              the greening hill,
              and violets
              that earth begets

# PLANTS AND ANIMALS

Just as water changes the rock base of the land, so do the thousands of living species that carpet and populate the Ozarks. Animals and plants that thrive in the temperate climate create the soil through decay of their waste products. At the same time they aid in the land's erosion. Animals eat the protecting cover and make paths down hillsides for surface water to travel. As it seeps through the vegetative debris, water becomes slightly acidic enabling it to gouge out valleys from the soluble limestone rock.

Photo 19
⇑ Indian Paint Brush decorates an Ozark glade, a semi-arid hillside where the rocks are too close to the surface to sustain trees.

Photo 20
⇒ Seeing the trees as obstacles to farming, early settlers cut down the forests which covered 70% of the land in Missouri. 1960 marked the low point of forested land. Replanting and letting nature have its way, have increased forested acreage.

Photo 21
⇐ Though usually associated with brush along fence rows, the sassafras tree can grow to great heights. This giant (on Missouri Highway 32 east of Lebanon) is reputed to be the largest in the world.

Photo 22
⇑ Many species of trees produce food palatable for animals and humans. After frost, these persimmons will make puddings, jams, breads, and cakes. Among the wild fruits are pawpaws, serviceberry, plum, and cherry. It is said that a persimmon seed will predict the weather. If the shape of a fork shows in the halved seed, the winter will be mild. A spoon predicts a hard one.

Photo 23
The Ozarks has more species of native plants than any other comparable area. Resistant, uneroded areas were covered with prairie grasses before the settlers plowed it under. Big and little bluestem, Indian grass (shown here), and switch grass were common varieties.

Photo 24
Though most of the prairie grasses are gone, prairie flowers such as these coneflowers find a home in pastures and along roadsides . . .

Photo 25
⇐ . . . and sunflowers thrive in the protection of fence rows.

Photo 26
⇑ The streams abound in animal life from microscopic organisms through fish, reptiles, birds, and mammals such as otter and beaver. A warm spring morning finds turtles sunning on a log . . .

Photo 27
. . . or ducks taking their morning swim . . .

Photo 28
. . . while a frog soaks up the sun that finds its way through the leafy canopy.

Photo 29
Almost hidden in the brush, the wild turkey comes to the edge of the woods to feed.

Photo 30
Cowering in the litter, this prairie meadow mouse freezes for the photographer before scurrying to the safety of its tunnel. By eating grasses, loosening the soil, and depositing its wastes directly into the soil, the tiny creature is an important link in the ecological system.

Photo 31
Darting from danger, this raccoon clings to the trunk, hoping his mottled coloring against the tree trunk will protect him.

Photo 32
Coyotes adapt well to changing environments. They feed on rodents, and as scavengers, they clean up their habitat by feeding on old, sick, or injured wild animals.

Photo 33
After the Ozarks became a part of the United States following the Louisiana Purchase of 1803, the land had to be marked with some system before any orderly settlement could occur in its wild reaches. As R. L. Elgin is doing with compass and link chain, surveyors began in 1815 to criss-cross the entire area. They waded through swamps and rivers and climbed forested hills and rocky bluffs to mark with witness trees and stones the perimeters of each square mile.

# TWO

# THE PEOPLE AND THE LAND

Photo 34
The natural gravel and rock in the soil makes this country road passable in wet weather. It ignores the hills as it follows the section line.

# THE PEOPLE AND THE LAND

The Ozarks is not characterized exclusively by its natural assets. A very important aspect, and its most recent advent, are the people who settled in the region. Though the French and Spanish explorers and traders were here as early as the late seventeenth century (the Indians long before that), the ancestry of present Ozarkians arrived soon after the Louisiana Purchase of 1803 opened the area to Americans. Compared to the billion-year-old rocks, their stay on the land has been no longer than the fall of a single drop of water.

Influenced by the land and giving it order while shaping it to their needs, the early settlers were isolated geographically. In their rugged land, they continued the traditions and life style handed down though generations of living in Appalachia and before that from their ancestry from the hill regions of the British Isles.

Though seemingly homogeneous with common ancestral and cultural backgrounds, the people were diverse. Blacks were brought with early settlers, and a few groups of freed slaves moved here after the Civil War. Many Germans immigrated directly to the region. There were some Italians, Poles, Swedes, French, and in more recent times, Amish, Mennonites, Asians, and Hispanics who have added to the culture while retaining their individuality. The hills separated the settlers, yet bound them together as did the self-sufficient life style all prized.

Just as water gradually shapes the rocks, so has the land fashioned the character of the people as they freely used its rocks, water, vegetation, and wildlife.

Photo 35
Though the river is a barrier, its flow is tapped to push the ferry across the Current River at Akers. Wires from the ferry that are attached to cables stretched across the river keep the craft from floating downstream. The force of the water against an underwater oarboard pushes the ferry across the river.

# USING ROCKS AND WATER

Rocks and water are not all powerful. Early and present day Ozarkians have spanned the rivers. They have cut the stubborn boulders and have delved into the depths of underground realms for water, minerals, and building material for their tools and structures. Throughout the years people have enjoyed using their know-how, strength, and endurance to master the elements. Sometimes they succeed. Sometimes not.

Photo 36
⇑ Though people attempt to make river crossings easier, sudden rainstorms can quickly cover low-water bridges like this one on the Osage Fork at Davis Mill.

Photo 37
⇒ This swinging bridge near Hermitage across the Pomme de Terre River is always safe from high water, if the driver is brave enough to cross it.

Photo 38
The advent of better cars and trucks demanded stable high-water bridges. Very few of these one-lane, wooden-floored bridges are still in use. Lambeth Bridge, built in 1908 across the Osage Fork River in southern Laclede County is now on the National Registry of Historic Places.

Photo 39
In spite of their experience on the river, their skill, and good equipment, these boys are at the whim of the current and an overhanging sycamore tree.

Photo 40
⇐ Harnessing the steady flow of a hillside spring furnishes reusable, non-polluting power. Directed through a flume, the water has for many years turned this overshot wheel at Zanoni Mill in Ozark County.

Photo 41
⇑ Sometimes natural sink holes like White Oak Pond south of Lebanon hold water, becoming natural ponds for the farmer's use.

Photo 42

Not all people are fortunate enough to have a spring or sinkhole pond to furnish water. They must drill wells. But to locate the spot where the water is, many people use someone like Bill York who has the talent to find underground streams. His freshly-cut, forked, peach stick twists in his hands as it points down when he walks across the stream.

Photo 43
A simple rope and pulley device mounted on a frame of poles cut from the woods helps the girls draw up three gallons of water from a drilled well.

Photo 44

⇐ Rock ground down to clay over the eons has many uses. Rick Purves uses clay from local caves to fashion pottery. Just as the Osages once did, he fires it in pits in the ground using dung as fuel.

Photo 45

⇑ A hated chore on an Ozark farm is picking up rocks in open areas used for gardens, crops, or pastures. This job is usually delegated to children. An old-timer who loved the region said that the Garden of Eden was in the Ozarks. "The reason Cain killed Abel," he said, "was because Abel wasn't picking up his share of the rocks."

Photo 46
In addition to stone fences and posts, the plentiful rocks made sturdy and attractive buildings. Mount Zion Baptist Church at Akers is constructed from native rock.

Photo 47
Rock blocks form the impermeable walls of this unusual one-man jail at Arrow Rock.

Photo 48
⇑ Just as rivers furnish fun and excitement for all ages, so do the rocky caves . . .

Photo 49
⇒ . . . though the squeamish will soon experience hard knocks on unprotected heads and clothing soaked and coated with gummy cave clay.

Photo 50

For those who understand their secrets, native plants have many uses. Ella Dunn dug roots early in the spring for her special tonic, designed to "build up the body's system, purify the blood, and clear up the complexion." She used sassafras, burdock, sarsaparilla, and mayapple roots with the bark of wild cherry and dogwood.

# USING PLANTS AND ANIMALS

Just as did the ancient Ozark Bluff Dwellers and the Osages, American settlers used the plentiful living resources of the Ozark Plateau. The abundance and variety of plants and animals helped assure their survival by furnishing food, medicines, heat, shelter, and badly needed cash to pay their taxes. Modern Ozarkians continue to harvest trees, wild herbs, greens, and fruit as well as to continue their long tradition of fishing, trapping, and hunting.

Photo 51
The most obvious use of trees was for buildings. Durable and built to last, many old log buildings still decorate the landscape.

Photo 52 and 53
Two different views show the details of notching the ends of the logs for a tighter fit. Spaces between logs were chinked with wood chips, mud, small rocks, and later, cement.

Photo 54 and 55
Trees also furnished the raw materials for riving shingles. A splitting maul, a froe (pictured), and a mallet are the tools used to split the sections of wood into individual shingles to roof a building.

Photo 56
Roy Gage's wagon holds a rank of firewood he delivered to his neighbors. "Them ponies ain't got no reverse. I can't back them nowhere," he said about his Shetland ponies he trained to pull the small wagon he built to fit their size.

Photo 57
To fence animals out of gardens and crops, early farmers utilized trees for splitting out rails. Hardwoods such as black oak, post oak, or white oak were favored because they split easily and lasted longer than softwoods.

Photo 58

During the early decades of the twentieth century, millions of hand-hewn ties from Ozark forests were shipped out to build the nation's railroads. "I used to be able pick one of these ties up and walk with it before I turned thirty-nine," said Tom Price as he hacked out a tie to exact measurements. "Now I'd sink plumb down to my knees."

Photo 59

⇑ Hybridized naturally from the raspberry and dewberry during the ice age, the wild blackberry is widespread throughout the region. It is often called the "black gold" of the Ozarks. Terry Brandt, like many other girls through the years, ignores the chiggers and the sharp briars to pick buckets of the flavorful fruit for cobblers, jams, and jellies.

Photo 60

⇒ The land's resources meet more than utilitarian purposes. People with artistic inclinations capture the beauty of the growing season for year-around enjoyment. Carefully dried and arranged, bright yellow foxtail grass and red crab grass blend well with the cattail heads, lotus pods, and leaves of dock and mullein.

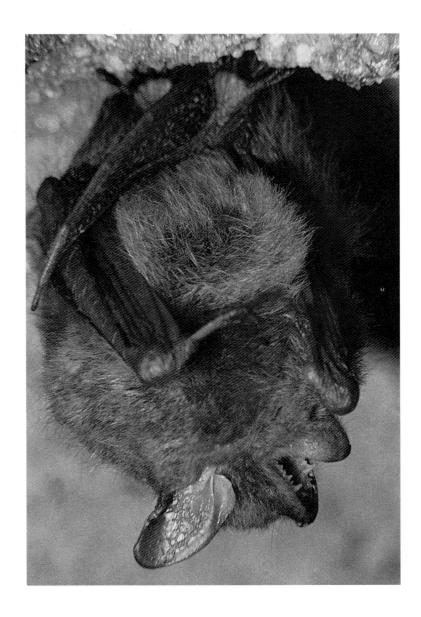

Photo 61

⇑ Brown bats like this one are prized for ridding the area of mosquitoes. Another bonus is their manure, or guano. "This is known as Bat Cave," Gene Chambers said. "It's well loaded with bats and the manure from them bats is the best fertilizer in the world. I hauled five loads out here one spring and put on our garden. We didn't notice much difference that year, but the next year—I mean that garden fairly went wild."

Photo 62

⇒ Honey bees were probably the first beings of Europeans descent to settle in the Ozarks. Brought to America by colonial settlers, some hives swarmed and became wild, spreading across the continent about a hundred miles ahead of the pioneers. Finding a bee tree, capturing the queen, and resettling the hive into a new home is still going on. And, of course, so is harvesting the golden, glistening honey.

Photo 63
When the work is done, many Ozarkians look forward to going fishing. Whether floating in johnboats or dangling a hook from a perch on the bank, men, women, and children enjoy the serenity while they hope for a bite. Fishing continues to be recreation that puts fresh meat on the table.

Photo 64
The catch from rivers have always been a source of needed cash. The first Europeans in the area were Frenchmen trading with the Osages for pelts. Early settlers continued trapping for income. Otter, mink, beaver, muskrat, and raccoon were all valuable for children to get money to buy school clothes and books. John Earl Kays and Keith Lundh continue the heritage.

Photo 65

⇐ A favorite sport for both men and hounds is to go 'coon hunting at night.

Photo 66

⇑ The opossum, also hunted at night, is prized for its pelt and for its meat. A special treat some people enjoy is baked 'possum with sweet potatoes.

Photo 67
"We have the best of both worlds." Lester and Rosemary Mondale's log home, furnished with hand-made furniture and wood-burning stoves, captures the charm of rustic Ozark life along with many of today's luxuries.

# PERSONALITIES ON THE LAND

As diverse as the landscape, men, women, boys, and girls call the Ozarks their home. Whether working, playing, or thinking about tomorrow, along with their families and neighbors, they are growing on the land as are the trees and grasses. Fresh and lively in youth, they become mellowed. Over the years the winds, sun, and rain chisel lines in their faces and round off shoulders. Like the meandering Ozark streams that move slowly to drain the Ozarks, their steps slow down. But always, even in the towns, they still smell the woods, hear the bubbling spring water, and feel the solid rock base at their feet, reminding them that the land was here first and will remain.

Photo 68

⇐ Neither woods nor tall grasses impede the young photographer in her efforts to capture her native land. Becky Baldwin admits, though, that she much prefers outings in the winter to avoid chiggers, ticks, and snakes.

Photo 69

⇑ Joe Jeffrey and Mary Schmalstig enjoy clear, fresh water from a farm yard pump.

Photo 70

⇑ "We call our acres on the creek [Crane] The Freshwater Biology Station. What my ambition is with respect to my research is to have a record of this kind of clear creek, which is getting rare in Missouri. Because I feel it is impossible for things not to change, my work will be to make some record of what it was like as it goes ahead with these changes that are inevitable," Dorothy Leake tells Carmen Broyles and Tracy Waterman.

Photo 71

⇒ "I'm not an expert on nothing, but when I could see, I could do pert'neer anything anyone else could. I could make a stagger on it." Wilford Haymes.

Photo 72

⇐ "I used to catch so many catfish they called me 'Catfish.' Also I used to catch a lot of crappie and they called me 'Crappie.' Then I had a kid working for me whose father called me 'Shorty.'" Olen Crews.

Photo 73

⇑ "My grandmother was a slave on a plantation near Pea Ridge, Arkansas. Blacks came with slave owners and some came after the war. They were free and they just wanted to get away." Gene McDowell.

Photo 74

⇑ "We both like farm work. We never hired anything done. He helped at the house, and I helped in the field. We've always got along good. Why, we just made a team." Letha and Sherman Webster.

Photo 75

⇒ "One day I saw six coyotes in a cow pasture. The country's full of them. They ain't afraid of you. You travel down the interstate and if you watch close you'll see a coyote sitting on the side of the road watching the cars. Most people see them and think they're dogs." Comer Owen.

Photo 76
⇑ "I always grow a beard in the winter. If I shave when it's cold weather, why then my face will freeze. It gets awful bushy, but I guess that's all right. People can't tell what I look like!" Norman Wright.

Photo 77
⇒ "I ain't as spry as I used to be. I built that barn out there when I was ninety-nine. That was the last work I done." Johnny Starnes at age 104 with his wife Esther.

Photo 78
"This bonnet here, I just washed it and put a little starch on it. It's just an everyday bonnet. If you wanted to run outside for something, then you just slip it on. Our mothers and grandmothers, they all worked outside and they had to wear bonnets on account of the hot sun. And on Sundays, why they'd have to have a nicer bonnet and they all seemed to like black." Annie Martin

# THREE

# THE CULTURE

Photo 79
When two musicians get together, they tune up and play. Out in the middle of the road is an unusual place, but who cares? Everyone listens and keep times when Bob Holt and Alva Dooms play old-time traditional tunes such as "Hooker's Hornpipe" or "Cotton Patch Rag." When asked if the big music stars at Branson play traditional music, Bob said, "It'd take a stone crusher and a lemon squeezer to get an ounce of tradition out of Branson."

# THE CULTURE

The culture of the people of the Ozarks is basically post-pioneer. They survived on the Ozark frontier as settlers did on other frontiers across the country when the population moved westward. What makes the Ozarks different from other regions, is that the life style did not materially change with new inventions, ideas, and morals, but continued through the middle of the twentieth century. Many aspects are still visible in the sixth and seventh generations. The survival of these customs is a major drawing card for visitors.

Until the invention of the automobile and construction of modern roads that easily scaled the hills and spanned the streams, people who lived in the Ozarks were isolated. Traveling great distances by horse power on mere trails with few bridges over the many streams was difficult. The westward moving world avoided the region for smoother terrain to the north or south.

Left alone, the settlers continued the way of life brought to America from the British Isles during Colonial days, sustained in the Appalachian Mountains for generations, and carried with them to the Ozarks. Cultivating on their 80 or 160 acre farms what the land did not provide, improvising and creating, the family was self-sufficient. They housed, clothed, and fed their families from the farm and the woods. They crafted tools, utensils, furniture, clothing, playthings, and decorations to meet their basic needs and appease their aesthetic natures. They had what they needed; very few had more.

Though isolated from the rest of the country, they were not isolated from their neighbors. They worked together on jobs needing more hands, such as threshing, siloing, or sorghum making. Small villages grew up on crossroads to service their more expanded needs. Stores, grist mills, blacksmiths, doctors, lawyers, schools, and churches were within easy access.

Life wasn't all work. There were social gatherings in addition to those organized to complete a job more quickly, such as quilting bees and barn raisings. Of prime importance was their religious and moral life. Because of living on individual farms, services and other activities held at the church, such as singing schools, were social occasions, a place for young people to meet.

Satisfied with their lives and resistant to change, the people continued their life style. They weren't ignorant of modern technological advances or recent ways of living and thinking; they simply were not interested. Their attitude can be summed up in two words—deliberately unprogressive.

Photo 80

After cutting down the trees, farmers planted fields for crops and pasture for the stock. The all-purpose barn, built of oak lumber cut from the farm, sheltered animals and stored the hay and grain necessary to survive the winter. The barn for the stock was as essential as a house for the family. When Rural Electric Cooperatives first serviced farmers, the barn was sometime wired before the house.

Photo 81

Most of the field crops were raised on small acreages and consumed on the farm. Grain binders and later combines were slow to gain acceptance. Because of the cost of the machinery, farmers continued well into the twentieth century to use the grain cradle to cut their small fields of wheat.

# ON THE FARM

The family farm, where once ninety percent of the population of the United States lived, is giving way all over the nation to corporate farming. Until recent years in the Ozarks, the family farm remained the basic economic and social unit. Its work ethic, economy, and the close family relationships continue to permeate the region. Still basically rural, the farm roots are firmly attached to the ground.

Photo 82
Even where the land is comparatively level such as this creek valley near Fredricktown, farmers have to contend with rocks and trees sprouting in cleared areas that aren't cultivated.

Photo 83
The richer plots of land become gardens or, in this case, a cane patch. Planting in May and thinning to one plant every foot by hand with a broad hoe is just the beginning in making sorghum molasses. Because of the amount of hard labor involved, very few families make their own sorghum now.

Photo 84

⇐ Every farm had an orchard and grape vines. People of French, Italian, and German descent planted grapes on the hillsides and developed a fine wine industry. Wines from some of the wineries rival those from California and Europe.

Photo 85

⇑ As late as the 1960s a threshing machine that serviced the farms in the community harvested the wheat and oats. Neighbors traded work with one another to get the twenty to thirty men needed for the harvest.

Photo 86
Corn was the most popular crop. This field is cut and shocked as farmers used to do. The versatile grain was fed to poultry, hogs, and cattle. When the grain was tender, the family ate it on the cob or canned it for winter meals. When mature, the they took sacks of shelled corn to the grist mill to be ground into meal for the ubiquitous cornbread.

Photo 87
The most efficient use of corn for feed was to use the whole plant. In the early fall, when the grain was in the stiff dough stage, farmers cut the stalk, ran it through a stationary cutter which blew it through a long pipe up into the wooden or concrete silo where the natural acids in the plant preserved it.

Photo 88
Using the land for pastures has always been profitable. Year after year the rich valleys and poorer hillsides furnish grass from early April through November. Beef cattle grow and fatten while dairy cattle turn the forage into milk . . .

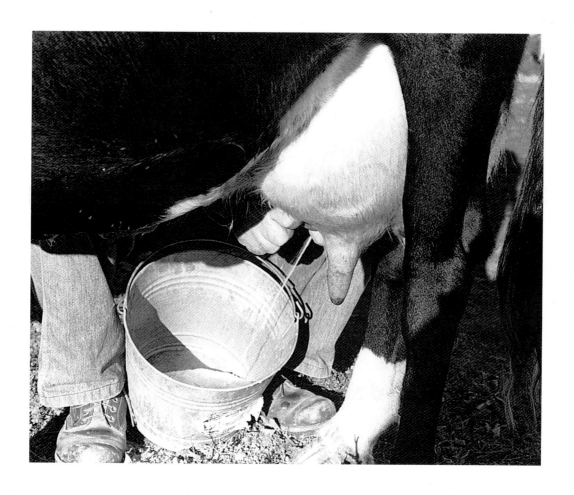

Photo 89

. . . that sings as it hits the sides of the metal bucket.

Photo 90

⇐ Perhaps the most important animals on the farm used to be the mules or horses that furnished the power to mow the pastures . . .

Photo 91

⇑ . . . or to pull wagons, and perform many other tasks. The mule is so important to Missouri history that in 1995 the state legislature named it Missouri's state animal.

Photo 92

⇑ "Horses are really smarter than people give them credit to be. Well, when you're breaking a young horse and if you don't know how, the horse is smarter than two-thirds of the people. Now that's the truth if I ever told it. They're smart enough to know how to not let them break them. People sometimes don't know what to do to break one that's that way. My experience is, if you ain't smarter than the horse, you're pretty well blowed up." Dutch Snyder with his Missouri Fox Trotting horse.

Photo 93

⇒ Every farm raised hogs for family use since the meat could be preserved by salting and smoking. Hogs foraged in the pastures and woods before fattened on corn for family use or for the market.

Photo 94
Sheep are valuable for their yearly wool crop which is sheared in the spring. Relieved of their heavy coat, the sheep jump and play when released from their "barber."

Photo 95

Sometimes used for their milk, as these pictured here, the greatest use of goats in the Ozarks is for control-
ling sprouts. To farm youngsters the next hated job to picking up rocks was cutting new growth from
around stumps and keeping brush from overtaking cleared areas. A herd of goats eats the young, unwanted
growth that cattle will not touch. After a few seasons pastures will be free of sprouts.

Photo 96
Tending to the poultry was usually the women's responsibility. Furnishing eggs, feathers, and fresh meat all year around, poultry also represented a source of income. The eggs usually paid for groceries and supplies needed from the general store.

Photo 97
Geese keep down weeds and act as sentinels, sounding an alarm when any visitor arrives. The soft down of geese and ducks was plucked to fill pillows and feather beds.

Photo 98

⇐ Both pet and valued worker, the farm dog saves farmers many steps. Stanley Ruble said, "I wouldn't take ten thousand dollars apiece for one. That's just what I think about them."

Photo 99

⇑ The cat earns its bowl of milk by ridding the farm of the mice and rats that damage the stored feed in the barns and other outbuildings.

Photo 100
"Things we stored in a cellar were very precious to us because it was our grocery store," said Lois Beard. The best part of it was that the food didn't cost money—just much labor to first raise the fruits and vegetables, and then gather, prepare, and can them ready for future meals.

# IN THE HOME

In March 1954 Mary Susan Brisco wrote *The Story of My Life*. In her own handwriting and spelling she summed up the self- sufficiency of the farm wife. "We was a large famly, and we allways had lots of meat and lard and all kinds of vegtabls ever day and dried fruit purservs and krout. We diden't have any thing much to buy much grocery with sometimes a few eggs or a lb. of butter. When we diden't have plenty of milk, we drank spice brush or sassafrace tea. Pa would say, 'I go down to woods store to get tea,' because it grew in woods."

Photo 101

⇑ Well into the 1970s and 1980s women like Sylvia Gunter preferred their wood cook stoves to electric or gas ones. "I wouldn't give my wood stove for a dozen gas stoves. I can cook a meal on that quicker than I could cook on the gas one. But I don't use it in the summer when it's hot."

Photo 102

⇒ Things change quickly now in the Ozarks and modern kids raised on electronics aren't familiar with old stand-bys like this old, slightly rusted wood cook stove. Genetta was surprised when she saw one for the first time. "I thought the stove was going to be made out of wood," she exclaimed.

Photo 103

⇐ The casserole dish of freshly butchered pork ribs, combined with vegetables, potatoes, and gravy and then topped with biscuits, makes a nutritious, satisfying meal, especially when served with sassafras tea and capped with wild blackberry dumplings. Lois Roper Beard produced all ingredients for the meal on her farm. "We didn't have a big variety, but we always just had plenty of what we had."

Photo 104

⇑ Grown in great quantities in the Ozarks, apples are still a favorite fruit. They are easily stored in straw-lined pits or in cellars. They can be preserved by drying, canning, or making cider and apple butter. There is no more refreshing drink than fresh apple cider right from the press. As cider ages it becomes vinegar.

Photo 105
After cooking and stirring apple butter in the copper kettle for eight hours, John Playter shook his head when asked if it was ready yet. "We'll let it cook just a little longer." When he placed a spoonful on a saucer and tilted it to one side, the apple butter held its shape. "Now it's ready!" he said.

Photo 106

Though the task of growing cane to make sorghum molasses is long and arduous, the result, golden, sweet molasses, is worth the effort for some. Several people gather for the day-long job. They feed cane stalks into the mill (background) to extract the juice. The greenish juice is poured into a five-sectional, copper pan where several workers monitor and stir the juice as it cooks. They move it through the sections until the expert at the end says it is done. That batch is removed while all the others are moved to the next section and raw juice is poured into the first.

Photo 107

⇐ Nothing in the home is wasted. After the hog is butchered and the meat cut up, the remnants are ground into sausage while the fat scraps are diced. Following the old tradition, Letha and Elmer Simpson are rendering the lard in an iron kettle.

Photo 108

⇑ While women were gardening, canning, and cooking for their families, they also took care of their children. In the early years of the twentieth century, the average woman had six to ten children, some of them not surviving to adulthood. Baby dresses were long, washing was difficult, and cloth for diapers scarce. "When I think of the work I used to do, I think, 'Oh, Lord!' But I just always kept everything going," said Mary Jane Hough.

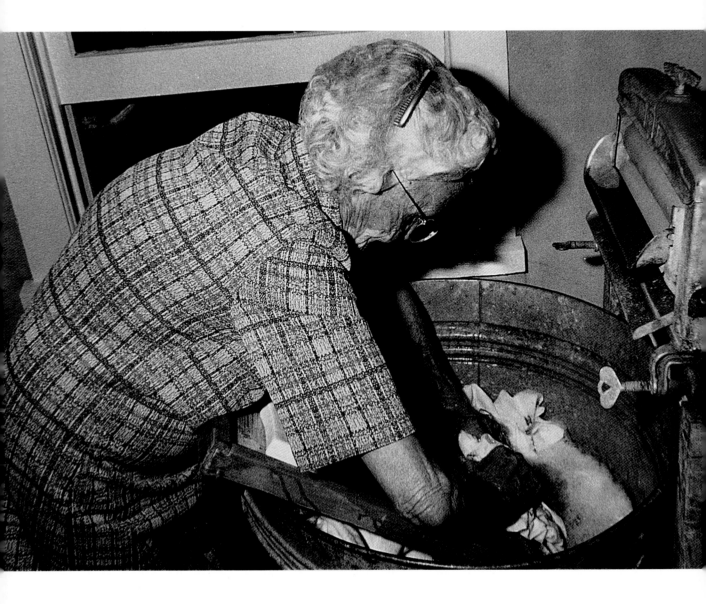

Photo 109

⇑ "I just did what had to be done. Whenever you make up your mind, you can do anything. When my husband died, I went to work. I washed clothes on the board for there was no other way then. I'm very particular about my washings. I've got an electric machine that was given me, but I never did use it. I wash yet on the board." Mary Ann Moore.

Photo 110

⇒ Hazel Cravens explained how to pluck the down and soft under-feathers from geese for stuffing pillows and feather beds. "You hold her feet as you pick. Put her head kind of behind your arm. You turn her down for obvious reasons, and then you pull the feathers out." Plucking doesn't hurt the duck. She's squalling because she's being held.

Photo 111
⇐ The first telephones came into the Ozarks in the 1890s when groups of about ten families shared the expense and effort to install lines. Farm people were no longer isolated but could visit with neighbors. Since the individual rings (two shorts, three longs) rang in all the houses, other people eavesdropped. If someone called late at night, all on the line listened for the call was sure to be an emergency needing their help.

Photo 112
⇑ Though old-timers are often nostalgic for the comfort of wood heat and the taste of home-produced and prepared food, not one misses the necessary trips to the outhouse. Electricity wasn't available during the 1940s, 1950s, and as late as 1960s in some areas. Even when they did have the power to pump water from deep wells, some farmers were slow to install indoor facilities in their homes. Some dairy farmers installed toilets in their milking barns before their houses since the plumbing was a requirement to sell Grade A milk.

Photo 113

The yearly overnight trip to the grist mill to get corn ground into meal and wheat into flour was an adventure to youngsters lucky enough to accompany their fathers. The three-story, wooden buildings hugged streams or springs that furnished the power to turn the wooden wheels or underwater steel turbines. Belts and pulleys throughout the structure powered the complicated machinery that ground the grain into human and animal food. Farmers enjoyed one another's company as they waited their turn. The miller took his "toll" for payment.

# OFF THE FARM

The bounty of the land and the people's ingenuity could not furnish all necessities. The family left their farms to trade their produce for supplies and custom work and to avail themselves of other services such as schools, doctors, and lawyers. Besides the economic need for the village, it also served a social purpose. Walter Niewald remembers his first trip to town when he was seven. "That was a big event that was a lot more than going to the world series now-a-days." But the twenty miles on poor roads was a long, exhausting trip. "We started out at two in the morning and got back at ten at night. And mud! It started raining on the way in and when we started back the mud was stiff. It was hard on your team when the mud sticks to your wheels."

Photo 114

⇐ The trip to town wasn't as long when automobiles became standard equipment in the hills during the early 1900s. But the machines brought different problems. Often the Model T was difficult to start as Gerry Darnell is discovering. "If anyone would drive thirty or forty miles and didn't have to clean a plug or two or patch a tire, he had a real news story to tell," said Walter Niewald.

Photo 115

⇑ Often the town was at a crossroads, or strung along the railroad tracks as Phillipsburg, shown here in 1974. A couple of general stores, a blacksmith ship, and a post office were obligatory.

Photo 116
With the advent of automobiles and good roads so that people could easily drive to town, country stores almost disappeared. Those that survived, such as Alloway's Store in Sleeper, kept up with the demand of modern customers. But they retained the bench in front for customers to relax or visit. Though mainly a business, country stores were also social centers where the farm people could catch up on the news, talk about their crops, or exchange recipes.

Photo 117
Behind the counter in this country store at Falcon, the storekeeper gathered items one by one as customers traded. Shelves that once held plow points, horse shoes, bolts of calico, overalls, and cans of lye, now hold Jell-O, Kool-Aid, and dishwashing detergent.

Photo 118
The United States Post Office was often a cubby hole or alcove in a corner of the store. The merchant, or his wife, was postmaster. This post office in the Falcon store has post office boxes accessible to the patrons. Formerly they asked the postmaster for their mail which he sorted into alphabetized slots behind the window.

Photo 119

"I've been in the shop all my life. But it wasn't easy. You make just as much as you want to make if you want to work hard enough. I wouldn't quit. This is my life right here. You know, it's a fact that you will rust out quicker than you'll wear out. I'm going to stay as long as I can stand up to use the hammer." Fred Manes.

Photo 120

⇐ Years ago all it cost for lumber to build a barn or a new room on the house was labor. Trees grew on the farm. The farmer cut them, hauled them to a sawmill or had the sawyer bring his portable mill to his farm. The sawyer received his payment in logs.

Photo 121

⇑ If the town was lucky, like Osceola, it had a doctor like Dr. Ruth Seevers. "Sometimes people used to walk to see me in the snow when they didn't have rubber footwear. They wrapped their feet in gunny sacks tied with strings. That kept them from slipping on the ice." At age ninety-one in 1974, she said she couldn't retire. "People would still come. What am I going to do? I've got the ability and the material at hand to help these folk. No, I can't retire."

Photo 122 and 123

⇐ Another needed service was that of a lawyer to help with legal problems. "If we didn't have any law, we wouldn't have anything but confusion. And we have enough confusion with the law anyway. I was the only lawyer in Conway. I had all the business I could handle." Spencer Legan.

Photo 124

⇑ Of prime importance was the school. One- or two-room schools were within walking distance—usually no farther than two miles. Hollen Mott taught one-room schools in Laclede County for thirty-eight years until 1973 when Missouri law closed all three-director districts. He saw many advantages of having students in eight grades together in one room. Younger ones learn from the recitation of upper grades while older children review by helping the younger ones.

Photo 125
Community gatherings such as this reunion at Dry and Dusty School often include a basket dinner of home-cooked food. The school was a popular gathering place for everybody.

Photo 126

A farm auction continues to attract people from miles, both to find bargains and to socialize. Whether selling off excess stock, machinery, and household goods or selling out an estate after death, the occasion is spirited. The air is full of excitement and anticipation as the auctioneer cries one item after another. Selling the stock is always last. Gerald Knight concludes a sale. "I've got five eighty. Five-five, eighty-five? Calf sold for eighty-five dollars a pair."

Photo 127

"I used to work against them and now I'm working fer them," said Art Patterson about federal revenue men while demonstrating the art of making whiskey at Ozark National Scenic Riverways at Alley Spring. "When they came to hire me, I said, 'It looks like a foolish idea, you people trying to hire me as many years as you've been a-running me.' They said, 'We've just decided we can hire you cheaper'n we can hire two revenue men to be after you all the time.'"

Photo 128

Neither the pigeon perched peacefully on top nor the fine craftsmanship of the native sandstone rock take away the eerie feel of the old jail in Nevada. Stony Lonesome was the nickname given it by former inmates. The name is doubly appropriate because on May 26, 1863 the stone jail was one of the half dozen building to survive the burning of the town by Captain Anderson Morton of the Federal Army, even though Missouri remained in the Union.

Photo 129
For recreation and as a means to get fresh meat for the family, guns continue to play a dual role in the Ozarks. Antique muzzle-loading, black-powder guns like this Hawken caplock were used by Ozark farmers up to the 1900s and longer. Today special hunting seasons are set for antique guns. Then and now people enjoyed and prized these guns.

# RECREATION

There were good times along with the work. After reciting how she raised pigs and calves, made head cheese [souse] from the snouts and jowls of hogs, made vinegar and ironed clothes with three flat irons, we asked Stella Muench if she ever had any fun. "Oh, yes. We used to have good times on the farm. They had pie suppers and dances in the community. We used to have baskets and fill them with flowers on May Day. We used to play jumping rope and hopscotch, king on the mountain and lie low sheep. We had a wonderful time."

Many of the good times involved all ages participating together in games, music, or dancing. Some of it was solitary such as fishing and hunting. But all helped to balance their lives—a sense of achievement crowned with time for fun.

Photo 130
The hunter's partner is his dog, which is usually specialized for different game, such as rabbit, fox, raccoon, or quail. In addition to the fun of hunting, owners sometimes show their dogs in bench and field trials. Stanley Arnold poses his prize foxhound, Hy Fashion.

Photo 131

Fox hunters never shoot the fox. Never. They want the fox to live so they can have a race another night. After turning their hounds loose, hunters relax on a hilltop to wait for the music to start—the music of the hounds who have caught the scent of a fox. The race is on. Each hunter recognizes the bark of his dogs, knowing which dog is in the lead. "I'd rather hear a good fox race than I would the Grand Ole Opera, and I'm fairly fond of that," said Stanley Arnold.

Photo 132
'Coon hunting, like fox hunting, is done at night, though the hunters want the 'coon for its pelt. Instead of running after the hounds over the rough, wooded hills, some hunters ride specially trained, jumping mules to follow the hounds. When the chase is blocked by a fence, the hunter dismounts, climbs the fence . . .

Photo 133
. . . the mule jumps over the fence, the hunter remounts, and follows the hounds.

Photo 134

⇐ For entertainment at home or at a gathering, no one is more popular than a good storyteller. Douglas Mahnkey tells true stories, such as the one about a new sheriff of Taney County who just swore in a deputy. "'Now Mr. Sheriff,' the deputy asked, 'if we get orders to capture a bad man, a real dangerous character, what shall we do?' Non-plused the good-hearted sheriff replied, 'Jest be careful and don't overtake him.'"

⇑ Photo 135 and line drawing 136
Young and old continue to attend singing schools to learn to read music and sing in harmony using shape notes. The shape of the note (triangle for do, round for sol, square for la) indicate if it is do, re, mi, fa, sol, la, or ti.

Photo 137

Among Charlie McMicken's leisure time activities was square dancing. Because some churches objected, he got a bad name over it for leading the children astray. "For all I know they may be right, but we've enjoyed it. It didn't hurt anybody. We've had a many a dance in our living room, and we'd take the stove pipe down and have a square dance. After it was over, put the stove back again until next time."

Photo 138
While the babies sleep on the bed, everyone has a good time. The old folks enjoy the music and the antics of the dancers as they go through the complicated figures. Charlie chants, "Ladies take a bow, Gents know how" . . .

Photo 139
. . . while Bill Fenton on the side lines claps and stomps to help the dancers keep in time. The square dance is Missouri's official state dance.

Photo 140
Accompanying himself on a ukelele his brother Jule made, Norman Wright strums and sings a little music
he heard in his youth.

Photo 141

⇐ Whipping his mountain dulcimer with a turkey quill as he notes it with a whittled down piece of a fence post, Bill Graves sings, "Oh Jesse had a wife to mourn for his life..." His name for the instrument his grandfather made during the Civil War is "Walking Cane" because it is so long and narrow.

Photo 142

⇑ "It's a ringer," Charlie Morgan says to his son Lowell standing forty feet away. The horseshoe clangs against the stake, hugging it for three points. In backyards, at the country store, or any place men congregate for a few minutes of leisure, someone will start a game. Four horseshoes and two stakes are all the equipment needed.

Photo 143

"Ball," shouts a player. At rural schools where there weren't enough children for two softball teams, they played "work up." When struck out, the batter retired to right field. To get his turn again at bat he had to work his way back through all the position as other players made outs.

Photo 144
Needing nothing but a small flat rock and a piece of ground, children enjoy playing hopscotch. Over the years new versions have developed, but the principle remains the same. Though painted on an asphalt playground here, children used to mark the pattern in the dirt with a stick.

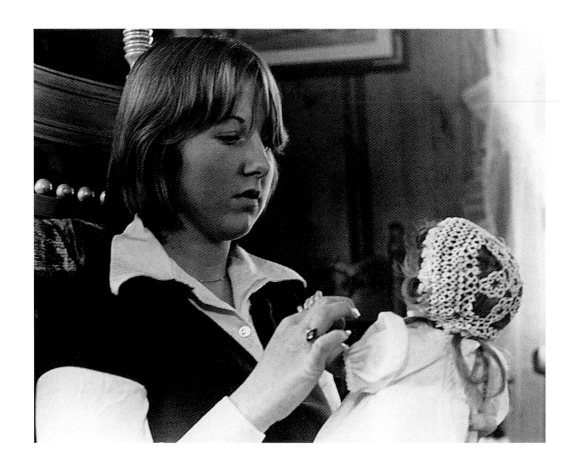

Photo 145
The appeal of dolls never completely disappears, even though most girls put them away. Patsy Watts can't resist holding this repaired and newly-dressed antique doll.

Photo 146
Stilts are easy to make from spare boards or sticks. Bird Elgin develops coordination as he walks on stilts his grandfather made.

Photo 147
Subsistence farming didn't mean there were no comforts or beautiful things in the homes. Ozarkians, like Elizabeth Fishwick, created beauty in many ways. Natural dyes from onions, goldenrod, mullein, sassafras, and wild cherry bark or roots turned colorless hand-spun wool into a rainbow of colors.

# CRATS

With very little money and stores often far away, men and women made do with what they had or could create from the raw materials available. They used the products of the woods and fields to make tools, furniture, boats, and decorations for their homes. They raised sheep and cotton for fabrics. Nothing was wasted. Decades before recycling was fashionable (or the term even used), they lived by the philosophy of the old adage, "Use it up, wear it out, make it do, or do without," by turning worn-out or discarded objects into something useful.

Needing bedding, the women made quilts from scraps too small for any other use. Furniture being essential, the men fashioned chairs from oak or hickory. Tired of drab colors, women created dyes from walnut hulls or marigold blossoms. Patchwork quilts developed into artistic patterns; small pieces of wood became carved ornaments to adorn the house.

Their creations we today call crafts. Born of necessity, Ozark crafts have survived. Today the biggest portion of the tourist dollar spent in the Ozarks is for crafts.

Photo 148
Sheared from sheep, the wool is cleaned and carded to straighten out the fibers before spinning into useable yarn. As some modern spinners, Carol Lee, uses a walking wheel her husband Carl made which was patterned after the wheels of pioneer days. The spinner steps back as she pulls out the wool rolag and forward as the turning spindle takes it up. While spinning, pioneer women might walk twenty miles a day from corner to corner of their cabins.

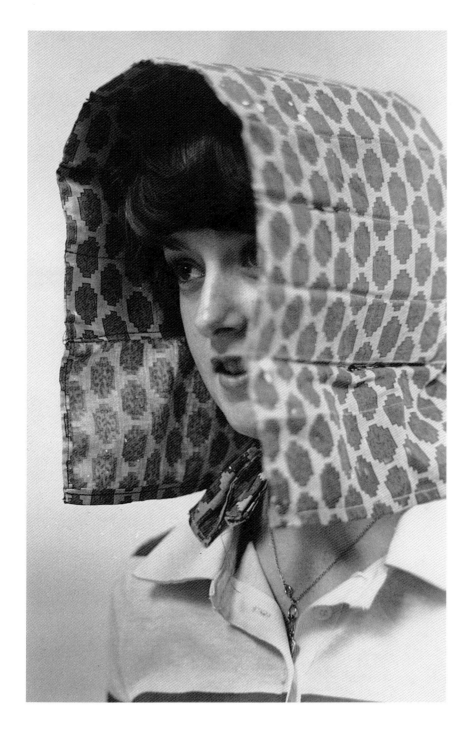

Photo 149
Next to preparing food, the next biggest task for women was sewing for their families. They used home-spun material, precious dress good purchased from the store, or reused the fabric from outgrown clothes. This split bonnet was made from feed sacks. Its brim is kept stiff by removable cardboard slats slipped into the sections of the brim.

Photo 150
Ray O'Dell is piecing into geometric shapes for a quilt top the small scraps of material left over from cutting out a garment. She has already reused faded and worn out garments to weave the rag rugs at her feet.

Photo 151
Thousands of tiny stitches running along the inside and outside edges of each little piece of this quilt will fasten the top, filling, and lining together. The finished product does more than keep sleepers warm. This Improved Nine Patch quilt becomes a work of art.

Photo 152

⇐ Strips torn or cut from rags, tacked together and rolled into balls are ready to be woven or crocheted into a multicolored rug. "I just use garments that are worn out that're really too good to throw away." Edith Fulford.

Photo 153

⇑ The hand-hewn, oaken loom, which Silas Barr built before 1857 for weaving rag rugs, has all its permanent parts fastened with wooden pegs. It is just as he built it with the exception of a new reed to replace the rusted original one and metal heddles in the harnesses to replace string ones. Succeeding generations of Ozarkians continue to weave as the Barr women did before the Civil War.

Photo 154

⇑ Huck weaving, or Swedish embroidery, is an example of a craft that has no practical purpose or need. A towel, dresser scarf, or pillow top is not made more functional by the decorative thread that is woven into the huck toweling with a tapestry needle. However, the artistic effect meets an aesthetic need for beautiful surroundings.

Photo 155

⇒ "It isn't work to me," said Roy Gage about his hickory bark chair seats. "It's more pleasure than anything else. I had a good trade making chairs. I could make about four a day, making the chairs and bottoming them. This ain't very hard to learn. Anyone could learn. I did and I'm not as smart as a lot of people."

Photo 156
"Making seats of corn shucks is a very old craft. It is an example of the pioneers making do with whatever was near at hand. We are told that the Indians taught the early settlers. It takes me about two days to do the seat of a chair working eight full hours. It is awful slow and awful tiresome on your hands and arms." Irene Haymes.

Photo 157 and 158

"Weave as many strips as you want to make the basket as tall as you want," Lyn Marble said as he wove the dampened, white oak strips into the size basket he wanted.

Photo 159

"I've made ropes ever since I was a child." Sam Schendel grew up on a farm where ropes were not always available. The equipment is simple—the winding board Jeff Zander holds and another board with three wire hooks connected to a handle which turns the three hooks at the same time (not shown). These hooks twist into a finished rope the rope-making material—rug yarn, sisal, or binder twine. As the handle twists the plies and Jeff holds taut the notched winding board, John Williams (not shown) pulls out the finished rope.

Photo 160
Early johnboats were built right on the river bank. Long and narrow to go through brush and around log jams, they were stable enough for a person to stand upright while fishing. They floated in four inches of water. First built for necessary transportation on the small, crooked Ozark streams, they continued as recreational fishing craft until the lighter, easier to maintain aluminum johnboats and canoes replaced them. Emmitt Massey prefers a wooden boat. "It don't make near the noise that a metal one does in the river. Also the wooden ones are actually easier to handle."

Photo 161

⇑ "My pictures all tell a story just as I remember about things that happened to me years ago. Here the horses were scared to death. You see the man driving the car is over just as close as he can be to the other side of the road. But the woman had to get out and hold the horse anyway, and they start backing up and almost turn the buggy over." Daisy Cook.

Photo 162

⇒ Fiddlin' 'round isn't just a waste of time to Violet Hensley. She not only plays the fiddle, but she makes them of cherry or maple. The fiddle is Missouri's official state instrument.

Photo 163
Nature seems to be in partnership with the people in seeing to it that this cemetery is decorated all year round. One of the most important days in the year has always been Decoration Day (Memorial Day). Strong family ties and the religious upbringing has made the hundreds of cemeteries throughout the Ozarks well loved and tended places.

# PHILOSOPHIES

Just as the Ozark people have held on to their way of life whenever possible, continuing the speech and old traditions their ancestors brought over from the British Isles, so have many retained their moral codes, their religion, and their philosophies based on love of family, hard work, and self-worth. They worshiped together when they could get to the local "meetin' house," but most of the time each person developed a truth or logic to live by, passing it on by example to the next generation.

Photo 164

⇐ Of high priority to the Ozark people is their religion. Baptist, Methodist, Christian, Presbyterian, and other Protestant churches are most numerous. Also, rural people didn't have to make the trip to town to attend. Country churches abound at crossroads such as the Lutheran Church at Morgan . . .

Photo 165

⇑. . . or the Cumberland Presbyterian Church out in the country in the Happy Home community in Webster County.

190

Photo 166

⇐ Religious gatherings weren't restricted to buildings. During the hot summer when there was a lull in the farm work and a traveling preacher visited the community, the men constructed a temporary shade from brush. To celebrate this era, the Church of God at Bennett Spring State Park recreated the brush arbor experience.

Photo 167

⇑ The tradition continues. Beside a modern highway in the Ozarks one still spots an occasional brush arbor where people congregate on a hot summer evening.

Photo 168

⇑ "Gone but not forgotten" is a favorite saying chiseled into many grave stones. This little boy's story has been preserved for several generations. The footstone of a boy who died of blood poisoning has the child's real hammer. Following his carpenter father, he stepped on a nail. His parents preserved his prized hammer, his birthday present.

Photo 169

⇒ "We used to sit up with and care for the dead 'cause we loved them. When they had the funeral there was lots of help. When everybody was there, that's all that was required. They took care of you when you died. Showed lots of respect. Prayed lots of prayers. Sang lots of good old-time songs." Mary Ann Moore.

Photo 170

⇐ "I was possibly seventeen or eighteen years old when I started singing for funerals. There was eight of us youngsters in the family and we all sang. They'd have the funeral in the church, then we'd go to the cemetery. We'd sing three or four songs while they were filling in the grave. All my life I've sung at funerals, first just in that community but after I got up in my twenties, why we'd go to different places. I've sung at five thousand funerals." Ashford Hough.

Photo 171

⇑ "I've really enjoyed life a lot. Back when I was growing up we had good times. Everybody had all they wanted to eat. We weren't dressed up, but we got there and back. I always said, 'If I had a good horse, a big hat and a pair of spurs and boots, I was on cloud nine!'" Emmett Adams

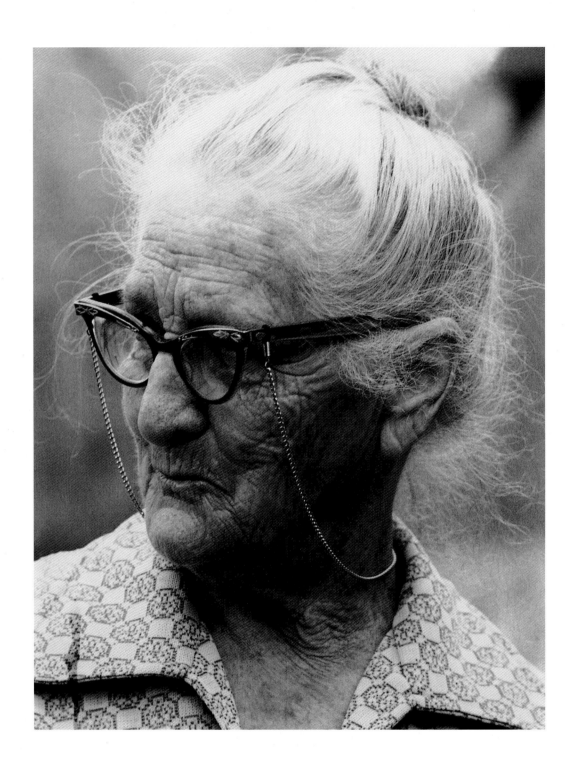

Photo 172
"Did you ever think of it, that that's why we are here? We're a diamond in the rough, and when the Lord rolls us around here enough that we're polished, He'll take us home." Ella Dunn.

Photo 173

"We didn't have the money and all the helpful things we have now. Like electricity. That is marvelous. I'd hate to do without electricity. I could, of course, but I'd hate to. I'd rather live in this day, wouldn't you? All of you folks are fortunate. You don't know how fortunate you are." Myrtle Hough.

Photo 174
"I've met a lot of people in my life. If I could live my life over, I might love a few more girls. The good Lord loves them all, why shouldn't I? After the life I've lived, I've never had a kid that caused me any trouble. I said, 'Don't do what Dad does, just do what Dad tells you to do.' And whatever you do, the best policy is honesty and truthfulness." Ike Fry.

Photo 175

"I've lived on a farm all my life. I learned to work and I appreciated it afterwards. I would help my husband plant potatoes. Well, that was no more than right. I would help him dig potatoes because I was afraid he would leave some of them. I spoilt him and he thought I had to help him with everything. I was ambitious and I went along." Katie Lowry.

Photo 176

"I never had a college education and I sure missed it as the years went on. So I was very insistent when it came to sending my children to school to get an education. And I encourage my granddaughters, too. If you have that, nobody can take it away from you." Bertie Rittershouse.

Photo 177

"I think a person should just be honest and true to convictions and always try to be a help to others, and I don't know what better advice I could give anybody to lead a good life than that. Because I think you get more enjoyment out of helping others than you could out of any other part of life." Charlie Grace.

Photo 178

"I think my generation was many more times contented than people are today. If I had my choice to grow up when I did or to grow up now with conveniences and luxuries, I'd take the old days. To me the standard of living is not how much you got, but how content you are with what you have and that you find real satisfaction in what you are doing. Now to me that is a standard of living. Contentment." Walter Niewald.

Photo 179
On November 16, 1939 Mary Elizabeth Mahnkey of Taney Country wrote this poem in her journal.

       To a Melancholy Lady

       Raise some guineas
       Raise some gourds
       Make a little gesture towards
       A richer life in service passed
       To leave some imprint that may last.

       If not great deeds
       Or golden words,
       Then raise some guineas
       Raise some gourds.

Photo 180
Footprints in the snow.

# EPILOGUE

The land and its people, that is the Ozarks. Just as water has carved out hollows and valleys from the rocky plateau to create the Ozarks, so has the land formed the character of the people. Using their own ingenuity and creativity, and with pride, wit, love, and respect, they have used what the land offers. They survived the hardships, the dangers, and the heartaches. With hard work, hope, and humor they have kept alive the spirit of the frontier. Pulsing with energy as never before, and finally after decades of ridicule, recognized by the rest of the world as a great place, the Ozarks and its people are blending the new industries, the ever-increasing tourism, and the influx of artists and retirees into their traditional life style.

This was how the American westward movement worked, men and women blazing new trails as they retained what they valued of the old. In the speech, philosophies, and activities of the Ozark people are preserved facets of the nation's past. This is our American heritage. The isolation of the area and the shunning by the rest of the nation for so many years have helped to save it.

And the future? Ozark folklorist Vance Randolph said in 1973 that he was wrong in thinking that the people he interviewed in the 1920s and 1930s were the last of their kind. Fifty years after his work, the boys and girls of *Bittersweet* showed that the culture continues. Visitors can see visible evidence all around them and they can relish it in the people if they care enough to become acquainted.

For there is a commonality to us all. Maybe the Ozark people's closeness to the land explains it. Our spring-fed rivers, the wooded hills, or the rolling prairies may give us something urban people have lost. We don't know. But with the land a part of us, we keep pushing on—working, loving, playing, hoping. Hoping that we have done our best, as did Mary Elizabeth Mahnkey in the 1930s when she wrote this poem.

> Perhaps sometime, somewhere, some place
> Beside a distant shining sea
> We may be judged not as we are
> But as we've tried to be.

Because for all of us in the Ozarks, fifth, sixth, or seventh generation Ozarkians, newcomers, or visitors, life is a bittersweet experience.

Photo 181

⇐ "I've had a long life and figure that death is something that comes to all of us. I don't care to die. I believe in a hereafter." Charlie Grace

Photo 182

⇑ The Old Red Mill at Alley Spring.

Photo 183

⇒ Bittersweet vine.

# APPENDIXES

# PAGE NOTES

(Unless otherwise noted, all young people in the photographs are Bittersweet students from Lebanon High School, Lebanon, Missouri and all photos unless noted are in Missouri.)

Cover    Carmen Broyles, Tracy Waterman, Dorothy Leake. Crane Creek near Aurora, October 13, 1979. Photo by Mary Schmalstig.

1. Mike Doolin and Stephen Ludwig on the Osage Fork River. June 2, 1976. Photo by Daniel Hough.

2. Jill Splan, Clarice Splan, James Heck. Bennett Spring. June 18, 1981. Photo by James Heck.

3. Photo by Robert McKenzie.

4. Niangua River near Ha Ha Tonka. Photo by James Heck.

5. Elephant Rocks State Park. Photo by Ellen Gray Massey.

6. Johnson's Shut-Ins. Photo by David G. Massey.

7. Osage Fork of the Gasconade River. Photo by Lisa Goss.

8. Natural bridge, Christian County. Photo by David G. Massey.

9. Photo by David G. Massey.

10. Photo by Mary Schmalstig.

11. Photo by David G. Massey.

12. Pittman Cave, Laclede County. April 1974. Photo by Stephen Hough.

13. Johnson's Sink, Laclede County. March 1974. Photo by Stephen Hough

14. Photo by David G. Massey.

15. Osage Fork River. Photo by David G. Massey.

16. Near Davis Mill Crossing, southern Laclede County. February 24, 1975. Photo by Jim Baldwin.

17A. Photo by David G. Massey.

17B. Photo by James Heck.

18. Wild verbena in eastern Laclede County, Missouri. April 1976. Photo by Doug Sharp.

19. Laclede County. Photo by David G. Massey.

20. Photo by Robert McKenzie.

21. Larry Doyle. On the Dale Wood farm. September 11, 1975. Photo by Mike Doolin.

22. Photo by Ellen Gray Massey.

23. Taberville Prairie. Photo courtesy of Miriam Gray.

24. Photo by Ellen Gray Massey.

25. Photo by Mary Schmalstig.

26. Osage Fork River, Laclede County. Photo by Daniel Hough.

27. Photo by David G. Massey.

28.     Photo by Doug Sharp.

29.     Photo by Doug Sharp.

30.     Photo by Donna Scott.

31.     Photo by Lace Collins.

32.     Photo by Melinda Stewart.

33.     R. L. Elgin of St. James using a 1859 brass vernier compass. June 13, 1982. Photo by James Heck.

34.     Laclede County. Photo by David G. Massey.

35.     Linda Lee and Euel Sutton, on the Current River at Akers. September 23, 1978. Photo by Ellen Gray Massey.

36.     Photo by Daniel Hough.

37.     Near Hermitage. Photo by Stephen Ludwig.

38.     Lambeth Bridge, southern Laclede County. Photo by Doug Sharp.

39.     Stephen Ludwig and Daniel Hough on the Osage Fork River. May 1976. Photo by Doug Sharp.

40.     Zanoni Mill. Photo by Ellen Gray Massey.

41.     Photo by Larry Doyle.

42.     Bill York of Stoutland. January, 4, 1978. Photo by Mary Schmalstig.

43.     Kathy Hawk and Kyra Gibson, at home of Goldie Campbell, Richland. March 17, 1977. Photo by Ruth Ellen Massey.

44.     Rick Purves of Lebanon. October 1981. Photo by James Heck.

45.     Photo by David G. Massey.

46.     Akers. Photo by Ellen Gray Massey.

47.     Arrow Rock. Photo by Ruth Ellen Massey.

48.     Ronnie Hough in Mud Cave, Laclede County. April 1974. Photo by Stephen Hough.

49.     Rita Saeger in Pittman Cave, Laclede County. April 15, 1974. Photo by Robert McKenzie.

50.     Ella Dunn, Walnut Shade. Behind her Terri Jones, Diana Foreman, and Carla Roberts. March 19, 1977. Photo by Ellen Gray Massey.

51.     On the Gee Chambers farm, southern Laclede County. Photo by Jim Baldwin.

52,53.  Left photo by Robert McKenzie. Right by David G. Massey.

54,55.  Art Corn of St. James, Missouri. November 1, 1980. Photos by Kathy Long.

56.     Roy Gage of Morgan. September 1973. Photo by Robert McKenzie.

57.     At Wilson's Creek Battlefield. Photo by Ruth Ellen Massey.

58.     Tom Price of Lebanon. September 15, 1977. Photo by Joe Jeffrey.

59.     Beverly Barber. July 14, 1976. Photo by Ruth Ellen Massey.

60.     Dried arrangement by Esther Griffin of Lebanon. Photo by Kathy Long.

61.     Bat Cave on Osage Fork River. Photo by Robert McKenzie.

62      Gene Chapman at Orla. April 13, 1980. Photo by Mary Schmalstig.

63.     Ellen Gray Massey and Emmitt Massey, Osage Fork River. August 21, 1973. Photo by Robert McKenzie.

64.     John Earl Kays and Keith Lundh of Richland. December 1977. Photo by Doug Sharp.

65.     Art Bryant on a coon hunt near Niangua. December 26, 1977. Photo by Doug Sharp.

66.     Photo by Doug Sharp.

67.     Lester and Rosemary Mondale and dog, Loki, near Fredricktown. October 28, 1978. Photo by Mary Schmalstig.

68.      Becky Baldwin. December 22, 1978. Photo by Lance Collins.

69.      Joe Jeffery and Mary Schmalstig at the Arnett Massey farm in southern Laclede County. April 18, 1978. Photo by Ruth Ellen Massey.

70.      Carmen Broyles, Dorothy Leake of Aurora and Tracy Waterman. October 13, 1979. Photo by Mary Schmalstig.

71.      Wilford Haymes, Conway. June 11, 1981. Photo by Allen Gage.

72.      Olin Crews of Lebanon. October 5, 1978. Photo by Lance Collins.

73.      Gene McDowell of Lebanon. May 26, 1978. Photo by Joe Jeffery.

74.      Letha and Sherman Webster of Lebanon. November 1980. Photo by Allen Gage.

75.      Comer Owen of Springfield. January 17, 1976. Photo by Stephen Ludwig.

76.      Norman Wright of Lynn. September 19, 1980. Photo by Allen Gage.

77.      Johnny and Esther Starnes of Brownfield. March 18, 1976. Photo by Doug Sharp.

78.      Annie Martin of Dixon and Terri Jones. September 16 1976. Photo by Ruth Ellen Massey.

79.      Bob Holt and Alvie Dooms of Ava. March 11, 1981. Photo by Allen Gage.

80.      Photo by Kathy Long.

81.      Elvie Hough of Orla. July 17, 1973. Photo by Doug Sharp.

82.      Near Fredricktown. Photo by John Shore.

83.      Robert McKenzie. July 5, 1973. Photo by Stephen Hough.

84.      Photo by Mary Schmalstig.

85.      Republic. September 1973. Photo by Ellen Gray Massey.

86.      Near Wheatland. Photo by Ellen Gray Massey.

87.      Mike Doolin. December 7, 1976. Photo by Ellen Gray Massey.

88.      Charley Brittain of Dixon. June 12, 1975. Photo by Larry Doyle.

89.      Fuget Garrison of Eldridge. April 5, 1975. Photo by Robert McKenzie.

92.      C.H. "Dutch" Snyder, Lebanon. January 1974. Photo by Ellen Gray Massey.

93.      Photo by Lance Collins.

94.      Alexa Hoke. March 8, 1975. Photo by Stephen Hough.

95.      Photo by Mary Schmalstig.

96.      Photo by Lee Ann Anderson.

97.      Photo by Doug Sharp.

98.      Stanley Ruble of Stoutland. June 1979. Photo by Mary Schmalstig.

99.      Photo by Ruth Ellen Massey

100.     Cellar of Lois Roper Beard of near Conway. Photo by Mark Elam.

101.     Sylvia Gunter, Lebanon. January 26, 1974. Photo by Stephen Hough.

102.     Sally Moore and Genetta Seeligman. March 3, 1974. Photo by Robert McKenzie.

103.     Lois Roper Beard of Conway and Deidra Morgan. February 3, 1981. Photo by Allen Gage.

104.     Esther Griffin, Lebanon. October 1973. Photo by Rick Bishop.

105.     John Playter, Bolivar. October 20, 1979. Photo by Mary Schmalstig.

106.     The Charles D. Hough family, neighbors, and Bittersweet staff on the Hough farm, Phillipsburg. October 18, 1975. Photo by Ellen Gray Massey.

107.     Letha and Elmer Simpson, Lebanon. December 18, 1973. Photo by Stephen Hough.

108.     Lindsay Shotts, Lebanon. January 8, 1982. Photo by Scott Jeffries.

109.     Mary Ann Moore, Phillipsburg. February 5, 1975. Photo by Stephen Hough.

110.     Hazel Cravens, Lebanon. July 3, 1973. Photo by Robert McKenzie.

111.     Harva Burns, Lebanon. June 18, 1980. Photo by Mike King.

112.     Outhouse on Warren Dampier farm, Eldridge. Photo by Vickie Hooper.

113.     Orla Mill, southern Laclede County on Osage Fork River. October 1974. Photo by Stephen Hough.

114.     Gerry Darnell. Walter Niewald is from New Haven. 1978. Photo by Mary Schmalstig.

115.     Photo by Stephen Hough.

116.     June 24, 1976. Photo by Emery Savage.

117.     Falcon Store. 1976. Photo by Emery Savage.

118      Falcon Store, Richland. 1976. Photo by Emery Savage.

119.     Fred Manes, Richland. July 17, 1974. Photo by Robert McKenzie.

120.     Republic. September 17, 1981. Photo by Allen Gage.

121.     Dr. Ruth Seevers and patient, Osceola. April 16, 1974. Photo by Suzanne Carr.

122, 123. Spencer Legan, Lebanon. June 23, 1976. Photo by Stephen Ludwig.

124.     Hollen Mott, teacher at Washington School, Laclede County. April 30, 1973. Photo by Robert McKenzie.

125.     April 12, 1973. Photo by Ronnie Hough.

126.     Gerald Knight and Phil Esther of Lebanon, crying the sale at Warren Dampier's farm, Eldridge. February 13, 1982. Photo by Ellen Gray Massey.

127.     Art Patterson, Summersville. June 13, 1974. Photo by Ellen Gray Massey.

128.     Bushwhacker Museum, Nevada. Photo by Ellen Gray Massey.

129.     Tom Knapp. January 3, 1983. Photo by Vickie Hooper.

130.     Stanley Allen, Lebanon. September 11, 1980. Photo by James Heck.

131.     Willa Jean and Ralph Usery and Dean Reagan of Lebanon on a hill near Bennett Spring. September 23, 1980. Photo by Dwayne Sherrer.

132, 133. Quentin Middleton, Niangua. December 26, 1977. Photos by Lance Collins.

134.     Douglas Mahnkey, Forsyth. September 16, 1981. Photo by Lisa Goss.

135.     Richard Nichols of Wayne, West Virginia, teacher at Lee's Summit Church of Christ Singing School near Lebanon. June 3, 1974. Photo by Robert McKenzie.

136.     Drawing of shape notes.

137.     Charlie McMicken and Ridge Runners of Richland with the Bittersweet staff. Charles and Inez Calton musicians. March 1, 1974. Photo by Robert McKenzie.

138.     Ridge Runners square dancers of Richland and Bittersweet staff. March 16, 1974. Photo by Robert McKenzie.

139.     Bill Fenton, Richland. March 16, 1974. Photo by Robert McKenzie.

140.     Norman Wright, Lynn. September 19, 1980. Photo by Allen Gage.

141.     Bill Graves, Phillipsburg. October 17, 1973. Photo by Ellen Gray Massey.

142.     Charlie Morgan in background and Lowell Morgan, Lebanon. February 25, 1982. Photo by Deidra Morgan.

143.     Children at Dry and Dusty one-room school, southern Laclede County. April 30, 1973. Photo by Robert McKenzie.

144.     Children at Donnelly Elementary School, Lebanon. March 8, 1977. Photo by Gala Morrow.

145.     Patsy Watts holding a doll from the collection of Alma Bates, Camdenton. December 10, 1977. Photo by Vickie Massey.

146.     Bird Elgin, St. James. September 26, 1981. Photo by James Heck.

147.     Elizabeth Fishwick, Steelville. October 18, 1974. Photo by Ellen Gray Massey.

148.     Carol Lee, Eldridge. March 8, 1975. Photo by Stephen Hough.

149.     Beverly Barber. March 30, 1977. Photo by Teresa Maddux.

150.     Ray O'Dell, Lebanon. May 25, 1976. Photo by Doug Sharp.

151.     Ladies at White Oak Pond Cumberland Presbyterian Church south of Lebanon. March 4, 1976. They are quilting on an Improved Nine Patch pattern. Photo by Ellen Gray Massey.

152.     Edith Fulford, Oakland. September 17, 1975. Photo by Ellen Gray Massey.

153.     Kyra Gibson, Edith Fulford of Oakland, Carla Roberts, and Diana Foreman. 1976. Photo by KODE-TV of Joplin.

154.     Photo by Allen Gage.

155.     Roy Gage of Morgan. September 4, 1973. Photo by Robert McKenzie.

156.     Irene Haymes, Conway. June 11, 1981. Photo by James Heck.

157, 158. Lyn Marble, Falcon. June 13, 1975. Photos by Doug Sharp.

159.     Sam Schendel of Rolla and Jeff Zander. September 9, 1982. Photo by Allen Gage.

160.     Emmitt Massey, Lebanon. Student shown is Ronnie Hough. July 5, 1973. Photo by Robert McKenzie.

161.     Daisy Cook, Republic. October 20, 1973. Photo by Robert McKenzie.

162.     Violet Hensley, Yellville, Arkansas. February 5, 1977. Photo by Stephen Ludwig.

163.     Lebanon City Cemetery. Photo by Doug Sharp.

164.     Photo taken February 19, 1975 at Morgan. The church has since been moved to the Shepherd of the Hills Farm near Branson because the architecture is similar to Harold Bell Wright's church in Lebanon where he was pastor from 1905-1907. Photo by Stephen Hough.

165.     Photo by Gina Hilton.

166.     June 22, 1979. Photo by Ellen Gray Massey.

167.     Near Brown Branch. July 17, 1974. Photo by Stephen Hough.

168.     Lebanon City Cemetery. April 25, 1975. Photo by Rick Bishop.

169.     Mary Ann Moore, Phillipsburg. February 5, 1975. Photo by Ellen Gray Massey.

170.     Ashford Hough, Lebanon. June 24, 1975. Photo by Ellen Gray Massey.

171.     Emmett Adams, Forsyth. July 15, 1982. Photo by Ellen Gray Massey.

172.     Ella Dunn, Walnut Shade. February 6, 1976. Photo by Doug Sharp.

173.     Myrtle Hough, Orla. November 21, 1975. Photo by Robert McKenzie.

174.     Ike Fry, Springfield. January 6, 1983. Photo by Vickie Hooper.

175.     Katie Lowry, Lebanon. June 1, 1977. Photo by Doug Sharp.

176.     Bertie Rittershouse of Springfield and Kirsten Ksara. January 30, 1982. Photo by Allen Gage.

177.     Charlie Grace, Lebanon. June 18, 1975. Photo by Doug Sharp.

178.     Walter Niewald, New Haven. 1978. Photo by Stephen Ludwig.

179.     Photo courtesy of Douglas Mahnkey.

180.     Bennett Spring State Park. January 3, 1977. Photo by Daniel Hough.

181.     Charlie Grace, Lebanon. June 18, 1975. Photo by Doug Sharp.

182.     Alley Spring Mill. Photo by Robert McKenzie.

183.     Bittersweet vine. Photo by Robert McKenzie.

184.     Double Wedding Ring quilt made by Ray O'Dell of Lebanon. Photo by Ellen Gray Massey.

185.     Photo by Robert McKenzie.

Photo 184
Double Wedding Ring quilt

# INDEX OF PEOPLE
(Names mentioned)

Photo 185
Sunrise in the Ozarks

# INDEX OF PHOTOGRAPHERS
Photograph Numbers

*Teacher/advisors and consultant